Editor
Erica N. Russikoff, M.A.

Illustrator
Kelly McMahon

Cover Artist
Barb Lorseyedi

Editor in Chief
Ina Massler Levin, M.A.

Creative Director
Karen J. Goldfluss, M.S. Ed.

Art Coordinator
Renée Christine Yates

Imaging
Ariyanna Simien

Publisher
Mary D. Smith, M.S. Ed.

Author
Debra J. Housel, M.S. Ed.

Teacher Created Resources, Inc.
12621 Western Avenue
Garden Grove, CA 92841
www.teachercreated.com
ISBN: 978-1-4206-3464-8

Reprinted, 2016
Made in U.S.A.

Teacher Created Resources

Table of Contents

Introduction

The old adage "practice makes perfect" can apply to your child and his or her education. The more practice and exposure your child has with concepts being taught in school, the more success he or she is likely to find. For many parents, knowing how to help their children may be frustrating because the resources may not be readily available. As a parent, it is also hard to know where to focus your efforts so that the extra practice your child receives at home supports what he or she is learning in school.

The complex task of writing requires time and lots of practice to master. A child's ability to write well begins with the ability to write sentences. *Practice Makes Perfect: Writing Sentences* uses step-by-step lessons to convey what a sentence is (and isn't), as well as the necessary components, capitalization, and punctuation. The lessons teach how to identify and fix both incomplete sentences (fragments) and run-on sentences. Most of all, the lessons show your child how to identify and then create clear, concise sentences. This book also includes three pages of assessment practice to help your child score well on standardized assessments.

The exercises included in this book meet or reinforce educational standards and objectives similar to the ones required by your state and school district for second graders:

- The student will use complete sentences in written compositions.
- The student will capitalize the first word of sentences.
- The student will use periods to end declarative and imperative sentences, question marks to end interrogative sentences, and exclamation points to end exclamatory sentences.
- The student will use a variety of sentence structures in written compositions.

How to Make the Most of This Book

- Set aside a specific place in your home to work on this book. Keep the necessary materials on hand.
- Determine a specific time of day to work on these practice pages to establish consistency. Look for times in your day or week that are conducive to practicing skills.
- Keep all practice sessions with your child positive and constructive. If your child becomes frustrated or tense, set the book aside and look for another time to practice.
- Do not force your child to perform or use this book as a punishment.
- Allow the child to use whatever writing instrument he or she prefers.
- Review and praise the work your child has done.
- Gently correct and explain errors, then give your child the opportunity to redo a page he or she did incorrectly.
- Have your child read aloud to you the sentences he or she creates. Reading aloud helps any writer to find omissions and to hear the writing's rhythm and flow (or lack thereof).
- Read aloud daily to your child, especially good literature by Caldecott or Newbery award-winning authors. Abundant research has shown that hearing fluent sentences will help your child to develop his or her own ability to write fluently.

Defining the Sentence

A sentence is a complete thought.

The boys laughed. Where is the book? Stop it. It's hot outside!

A phrase is not a complete thought. This means it is not a sentence.

Sitting on a fence. When is the? The roses. Your house!

A sentence has one of four purposes:

to *tell*: I like to play catch.

to *ask*: Would you like to eat lunch?

to *order*: Please brush your teeth.

to *shout*: That's the most beautiful rainbow ever!

Directions: Read each set of words. Then, mark it as one of the following:

Telling sentence **A**sking sentence **O**rdering sentence

Shouting sentence **N**ot a sentence

Example: A What time should we come to your house?

_______ 1. Please watch where you are going.

_______ 2. In the basket.

_______ 3. Where did you leave the note?

_______ 4. My dad went to the store.

_______ 5. Finish your homework.

_______ 6. We have to hurry!

_______ 7. Each phone in our home.

_______ 8. It was October 6.

_______ 9. I want to play at the park!

_______ 10. How did she unlock the chest?

Defining the Sentence

Directions: Read each set of words. Then, mark it as one of the following:

Telling sentence　　**A**sking sentence　　**O**rdering sentence

Shouting sentence　　**N**ot a sentence

Example: T A lot of birds fly south for the winter.

_______ 1. Since Ann joined our class.

_______ 2. Mrs. Horn told her students to get out their crayons.

_______ 3. How many days are left before you move?

_______ 4. Get out of the way!

_______ 5. This food is delicious!

_______ 6. Do not open that!

_______ 7. These papers look old.

_______ 8. When is your birthday?

_______ 9. I love your laugh!

_______ 10. As we talked.

Directions: Write a sentence to . . .

tell your favorite color: ______________________________________

____

ask for a ride to school: ______________________________________

____

order your brother or sister to stop bugging you: ______________________

____

Exploring Four Kinds of Sentences

There are four kinds of sentences.

A sentence can make a **statement.**

The bus is coming. I want a black jacket. They own a store.

A sentence can ask a **question**. This kind of sentence can have just one word.

Where did she hide it? Will you come play with me? What?

A sentence can be a **command** or a **polite request**. The word *you* is not usually used. Still, you know that the command is directed at you.

Close the door. Stop talking! Please give me some food.

A sentence can be an **exclamation** (shout).

It's my birthday! He won the spelling bee! What a cute puppy!

Directions: On the line, write the letter for the kind of sentence each one is.

Statement **Q**uestion **C**ommand/Request **E**xclamation

_______ 1. Who moved into the house next door?

_______ 2. Please come in.

_______ 3. I can't believe it!

_______ 4. He is baking a cake for you.

_______ 5. You should come to my party!

_______ 6. Do not open that door!

_______ 7. Where is my red hat?

_______ 8. I am going to eat lunch now.

Exploring Four Kinds of Sentences

Directions: Read each sentence. Then, write the number of the sentence in the shape that matches the sentence type. The first one has been done for you.

1. Put your socks on.
2. Why are you sitting here?
3. He would like an apple.
4. It's falling!
5. Please answer the phone.
6. Last night my dad brought home a dog.
7. No! I won't do it!
8. What will you name your cat?

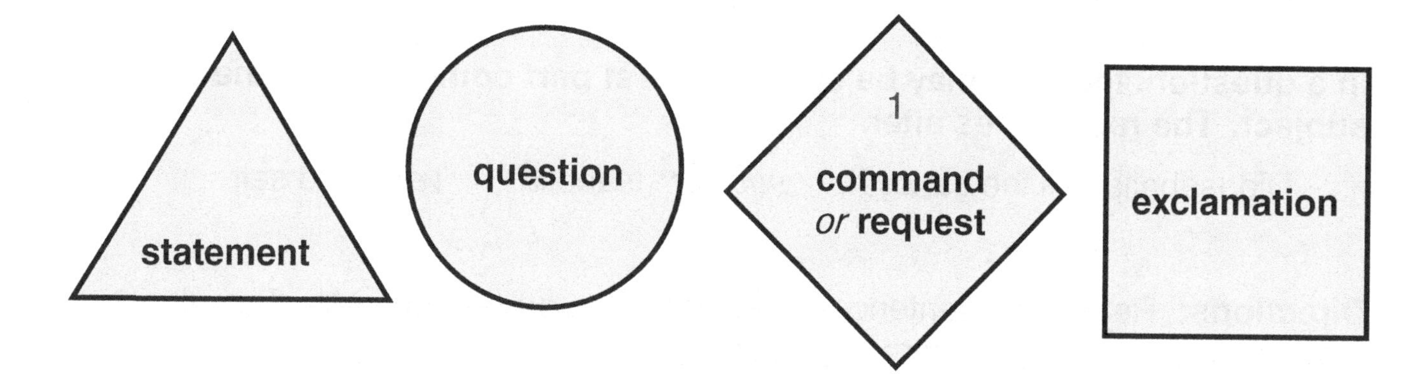

Directions: Write a sentence to . . .

tell where you live: ______________________________

____

ask a friend to play a board game: ______________________

____

command a person to pick up toys: ______________________

____

shout out who you like: ___________________________

____

Discovering Subjects and Verbs

A sentence has a subject. The subject can be a noun (*person, place, thing,* or *idea*). Or, it can be a pronoun (*I, we, you, he, she, it, they*).

A sentence has a verb. The verb may say what the subject does/did. Or, it may tell about the subject.

Tasha walked to school.	*subject:* Tasha	*verb:* walked
He is a nice boy.	*subject:* He	*verb:* is

When a sentence is a command, the subject may not be included. The subject is *you*.

Draw a picture.	*subject:* You	*verb:* draw

In a question, the verb may be split. The first part comes before the subject. The rest comes after.

Did Isabella sell the candy?	*subject:* Isabella	*verb:* did sell

Directions: Read each sentence. Underline the verb(s) and circle the subject. If the subject is not stated, write *You* at the end.

Examples: When did the dog run through the field?

Carry this bag. You

1. Ben opened the door.
2. Did you go to the fair?
3. Call the dog.
4. Shut the windows.
5. Sara laid the book on her bed.
6. Fairport is one of the towns along the river.

Discovering Subjects and Verbs

Directions: Read each sentence. Underline the verb and circle the subject. If the subject is not stated, write *You* at the end.

Examples: Where did that money come from?

Shut off the stove. You

1. We raced toward the finish line.
2. What did Bailey say?
3. They sang loudly.
4. A thick forest blocked our view of the shore.
5. Did Dan watch a movie?
6. Turn down the TV.
7. Liz pulled a chair up to the table.
8. I just saw a falling star!
9. They slept well last night.
10. Does she like it?
11. Eat up!
12. Sit down over there.
13. Your shoe is dirty.
14. Did you read the book?
15. Make some hot cocoa.

Making Subjects and Verbs Agree

Subjects and their verbs must agree. A singular subject means *one*. It needs a singular verb.

The *mother rocks* her baby.

A plural subject means *more than one*. It needs a plural verb.

The *mothers rock* their babies.

The letter *s* often appears at the end of the subject *or* the verb but not both in the same sentence:

The *boy walks* to the park. (singular subject, singular verb)

The *boys walk* to the park. (plural subject, plural verb)

Sometimes the singular subject is one thing made up of a lot of things. *A herd of cows* is one herd made up of many cows. *A flock of birds* is one flock made up of many birds. *Herd* and *flock* are both singular.

The *group* of children shouts for joy. (one group with more than one child)

The *pack* of dogs runs to its owner. (one group with more than one dog)

Directions: Read each sentence. Write **S** if the subject is singular. Write **P** if the subject is plural.

Example: S A girl eats a cookie.

_______ 1. The men stop for lunch every day.

_______ 2. The class is reading a book by Beverly Cleary.

_______ 3. That child looks lost.

_______ 4. My step team practices on Monday.

_______ 5. Her books fall off the desk daily.

_______ 6. The crowd of students tried to get out of the way.

_______ 7. Most dogs bark when someone walks by outdoors.

_______ 8. Monkeys swing from branches.

Making Subjects and Verbs Agree

Directions: Read each sentence. Do the subject and verb agree? If they do, write **A** on the line. If they do not, write **D** on the line.

Example: D The man drop a paper every day.

________ 1. Did you hides the key?

________ 2. Jack hates to eat corn.

________ 3. Spiders spin their webs.

________ 4. She sit on the dock.

________ 5. Does he sings like a rock star?

________ 6. I like to go to the store.

________ 7. That look like a worm.

________ 8. Did the kitten fall asleep?

Directions: Look at the chart. Choose the verb form that agrees with the subject given. Write a sentence using the subject and verb. The first one has been done for you.

Subject	Verb	Sentence
boys	talk(s)	The boys talk to their sister.
she	write(s)	
they	stop(s)	
we	like(s)	
flock	rest(s)	
mother	laugh(s)	
cats	purr(s)	

Using More Than One Subject

Some sentences have more than one subject (compound subject).

Songs and poems sometimes rhyme.

compound subject: songs, poems *verb:* rhyme

Did Tom or Jan read the book?

compound subject: Tom, Jan *verb:* did read

Compound subjects let the writer say the same thing about more than one person, place, thing, or idea.

Jack and Sara live in Greenwood. (one sentence, compound subject)

Jack lives in Greenwood. Sara lives in Greenwood. (two sentences, two subjects)

Notice how the verb changed. It is *lives* in each of the two sentences. It is *live* in the one sentence. Why? The verb must agree with two people instead of just one.

Directions: Read the two sentences. Then, write one sentence with a compound subject.

Example: Jenna plays the flute. Robin plays the flute, too.

Jenna and Robin play the flute.

1. Music CDs can be checked out from the library. DVDs can be checked out as well.

____

2. Where is my pencil? Where is my paper?

____

3. Kara likes to play with trucks. Tim likes to play with trucks, too.

____

4. Did Jim come home late? Did Megan come home late?

____

5. My sister ran in the race. My brother ran in the same race.

____

Using More Than One Subject

Directions: Add a compound subject to each sentence below. If the compound subject begins the sentence, use a capital letter.

Example: The rain and wind slowed us down.
(The compound subject is *rain* and *wind*.)

1. Both ______________________________ got done early.
2. Were ______________________________ planning to go to his party?
3. ______________________________ are good friends with Rico.
4. My ______________________________ bought me a new bike.
5. ______________________________ are three years old.
6. How did ______________________________ find their way out?
7. His ______________________________ enjoy playing chess.
8. ______________________________ were born in March.
9. The ______________________________ are in the cabinet.
10. What happened to her ______________________________ ?
11. ______________________________ own cell phones.
12. The ______________________________ are far from Earth.
13. ______________________________ are my two favorite sports.
14. Conner's ______________________________ got hurt in the crash.
15. Where did ______________________________ go last night?

Using More Than One Verb

Some sentences have two verbs.

Jon ran to the corner and rang the bell.

subject: Jon *compound verb:* ran, rang

Sentences use more than one verb to show more than one action.

Cory will make the meal and wash the dishes.

subject: Cory *compound verb:* will make, wash

Directions: Read the two sentences. Then, write one sentence using two verbs.

Example: Andi sings. Andi plays the drums.

Andi sings and plays the drums.

1. Zack cleared the table. Zack set the table.

   ____

2. Will Jill rake the yard? Will Jill trim the bushes?

   ____

3. Josh tripped on a root. Josh dropped the bag.

   ____

4. Did Karli feed the dog? Did Karli walk the dog?

   ____

5. Mason ran to the door. He opened the door.

   ____

6. Matt sat down. Matt played the game.

   ____

Using More Than One Verb

Directions: Circle both verbs.

Example: Water (picks) up dirt and (carries) it into streams and rivers.

1. Will Candi cook and serve the meal?
2. The tree branch snapped and crashed to the ground.
3. I ate a meal but still feel hungry!
4. The woman smiled and waved at them.
5. People stopped and watched the boy on the skateboard.
6. Can you sing and skip rope at the same time?

Directions: Write a sentence using both verbs given.

Example: swam and played Dana swam and played at the beach.

1. caught and threw

____

2. cook and bake

____

3. turned and ran

____

4. laughed and clapped

____

5. stood and stared

____

6. wash and brush

____

Spotting Sentence Parts: Articles

A sentence can have two words. One must be a subject and the other a verb.

He smiled. Laura nodded. I fell. It's cold.

Few sentences are that short. Many sentences have other words in them, like the articles *a*, *an*, or *the*.

A bird sang in *the* tree. *An* umbrella is on *the* desk. *The* door was open.

When a word after the article starts with a vowel (*a, e, i, o, u*) or vowel sound, use *an*.

The wagon sat next to *an* old barn. She picked up *an* egg.

Use *the* to refer to a specific thing. Use *a* or *an* to refer to something in general.

Let's go to *the* art shop. (a specific art shop)
Let's go to *an* art shop. (any art shop)

***A* or *an* are singular. Use *the* with plurals.**

A car pulled up to the stop sign. *The cars* pulled up to the stop sign.

Directions: Read each sentence and underline the articles. Some sentences have more than one.

Example: The teacher put a rug on the floor.

1. Please do not put the box on that chair.
2. I wish you could come with me to the party.
3. Do you have the book that Matt lent you?
4. An apple pie was on the table.
5. Let's buy an ice cream cone after the show ends.
6. A boat was tied to the dock.
7. The new toy was broken in less than two days.
8. Where do you keep the forks?
9. Step on the gas!
10. An axe was lying on the ground.

Spotting Sentence Parts: Articles

Articles

a an the

Directions: Read each sentence. The missing words are articles. Pick articles from the box above and fill in the blanks to complete the sentences. They must make sense. If the article starts the sentence, capitalize it.

1. __________ dog chewed on __________ old bone.
2. Will you come to __________ library with me?
3. After all __________ leaves fell, we raked them into __________ big pile.
4. I went on __________ field trip to __________ apple orchard.
5. We built __________ snowman in __________ front yard.
6. __________ animal had dug __________ hole by __________ bush.
7. Frank tried to find __________ exit.
8. She gets paid on __________ first day of each month.
9. You need __________ egg to make this cake.
10. What time of day did __________ fire start?
11. __________ boy was happy to get __________ gift.
12. He can open the lock with __________ key.
13. Take __________ clothes out of __________ dryer.
14. Is __________ cat hiding under __________ bed?
15. Jack found __________ cell phone in __________ ditch.

Spotting Sentence Parts: Prepositions

Many sentences have prepositions. Prepositions are short words. They join words or phrases. Below is a list of common prepositions:

of	by	as	up	with	from	after	near
on	in	at	to	under	about	into	above

Some sentences have more than one preposition.

We got *into* the boat *after* the storm ended.

A preposition tells where or when.

The game was *in* the cupboard *under* the blankets. (tell where)

On Friday night, we had dinner *at* EJ's Eatery. (tell when, where)

Prepositions are short, yet they are important. They make a sentence flow. If a sentence starts with a preposition, the word must be capitalized.

Directions: Read each sentence. Underline the prepositions. Most sentences have more than one.

Example: We are going <u>to</u> the carnival <u>on</u> Saturday.

1. We sat on a bench in the park after the wedding.
2. Of all the songs we sang, I liked that one the best.
3. Pick up the plates and put them by the sink.
4. The cat was lying above the chair.
5. She was named after her mother.
6. Ali went to the store with Jen.
7. At the museum, Cody got a poster about jets.
8. The farmer put the pig back into its pen.

Spotting Sentence Parts: Prepositions

of	by	up	with	from	about
on	in	at	to	under	into

Directions: Read each sentence. The missing words are prepositions. Pick prepositions from the box above, and fill in the blanks to complete the sentences. They must make sense. If the preposition starts the sentence, capitalize it. Each preposition is used once. Cross it off after you use it.

Example: Near the shore was a small shack.

1. ____________ the pile of books, I found the paper.
2. Please put this dish ____________ on the top shelf.
3. Ian took a cookie ____________ the tray.
4. The toy came ____________ a little box.
5. They went fishing ____________ Abigail.
6. Stop ____________ the corner.
7. Liza put the letter ____________ the mailbox.
8. Stand over there ____________ Ana.
9. The room is painted a shade ____________ blue.
10. Turn ____________ the computer.
11. Alex did not hear ____________ the sale until it was over.
12. The basketball player grew ____________ be seven feet tall.

Spotting Sentence Parts: Adjectives

An adjective is a word that tells about a noun. It describes the noun.

Sentence without adjectives: The boy sat on the dock.

Sentence with adjectives: The small boy sat on the wet dock.

Which sentence is more interesting? Which one gives more information?

Which one helps you to picture the boy and the dock?

Adjectives make a sentence better. But, do not overdo it. A few adjectives are better than too many.

Directions: There is one adjective in each sentence. Find it and underline it.

Example: She has a large dog.

1. My older brother plays football.
2. I wore a blue wig with my costume.
3. Did you see that striped car?
4. We watched a great movie on Saturday.
5. His little sister sings in the chorus.
6. Seth is the third child in the family.
7. Is Mrs. Frank a short woman?
8. I asked for a new skateboard for my birthday.
9. Those socks are ugly!
10. Clouds filled the dark sky.
11. What is the biggest box you have?
12. Look at that cute puppy!

Spotting Sentence Parts: Adjectives

Directions: A caret (^) lets you know that you need to add a word. At each caret, add an adjective.

green
Example: I like to eat ^ beans.
(Lots of adjectives could work: *wax, baked, navy, chili, kidney,* etc.)

1. Isabella needs to wash her ^ hands.
2. The ^ boy ran fast.
3. The dessert she likes best is ^ pie.
4. A ^ bird perched nearby.
5. The ^ dog followed me home.
6. Abigail ate her ^ potatoes slowly.
7. Jose asked for a glass of ^ juice.
8. A ^ girl screamed.
9. Our ^ door was open.
10. Where is the baby's ^ hat?
11. That ^ pan is hot!
12. Zack was the ^ boy in the class.
13. The ^ tree branch snapped and fell.
14. Smoke rose from the chimney of the ^ house.
15. My ^ arm hurt so much that I could not move it.

Figuring Out Word Order

You do not always speak or think in sentences, but you often do. When you form a sentence, say it aloud. (You can use a whisper.) Hearing the words will help you to figure out if it is a sentence and if the words are in the right order.

Sometimes the same words can make a statement or a question. It depends on the order in which the words are written.

Directions: Read each set of words. Put the words in order to form a sentence. Write it on the line. When you see (*ask*), make the sentence a question.

Example: the should to I store and Abe go (*ask*)

Should Abe and I go to the store?

1. your tall is grandpa (*ask*)

____

2. has he nose big a

____

3. not pan the warm was frying

____

4. time is to it already go

____

5. run did boy that fast (*ask*)

____

6. comes this which after book one (*ask*)

____

7. hard wind blew the

____

8. name his is what (*ask*)

____

Figuring Out Word Order

Directions: Put the words in order to form a sentence. Write it on the line. When you see (*ask*), make the sentence a question.

1. meat ate we rice and

   ____

2. did what you say just (*ask*)

   ____

3. she arm did her cut how (*ask*)

   ____

4. to able you tame bird wild were the

   ____

5. like you sister meet to would my (*ask*)

   ____

6. the came class she to early

   ____

7. fix dad the did broken his wheel (*ask*)

   ____

8. home came they yesterday

   ____

9. run printer my ink of out has

   ____

10. den is the yellow color the of

    ____

11. you book read by the yourself did (*ask*)

    ____

12. this won he race afternoon the

    ____

Beginning Sentences with Capital Letters

A sentence always starts with a capital letter.

The boat moved closer to the shore. **A** stray cat sat near the trash can.

In these examples, the first word in each sentence is a small word. The length of the word does not matter. If it is the first word, it must be capitalized.

Directions: Add a first word to each sentence below. Use a capital letter.

Example: My puppy has learned to walk on a leash.

1. ______________ wind blew so hard that a tree fell down.
2. ______________ will bake some cookies.
3. ______________ year I was in first grade.
4. ______________ book is due on Friday.
5. ______________ help me to study math.
6. ______________ will fly a kite.
7. ______________ you like to meet my brother?
8. ______________ mom fixed the broken pipe.
9. ______________ Dad say "yes" or "no"?
10. ______________ the bus already come?
11. ______________ go for a walk.
12. ______________ look like you need some dry clothes!
13. ______________ stop the bike, press the hand brake.
14. ______________ that your coat over there?
15. ______________ year I will be in third grade.

Beginning Sentences with Capital Letters

many	that	each	do	few
what	where	we	please	he
look	my	have	when	how

Directions: Pick the word from the box to complete each sentence. Write it on the line with a capital letter. To help you pick the right word, a word may be italicized (slanted) in the sentence. Use each word once.

1. _______________ loud noise is making my head hurt and my ears ring.
2. _______________ not touch that hot burner!
3. _______________ is wrong with the stove?
4. _______________ raced to the river to save *our* friend.
5. _______________ they reached the corner, Joe turned left.
6. _______________ new room is painted a nice shade of green.
7. _______________ people live in the Arctic.
8. _______________ saw a shooting star last night.
9. _______________ did you get the door unlocked?
10. _______________ you met my sister?
11. _______________ out below!
12. _______________ help me to lift this heavy chair.
13. _______________ are my mittens?
14. _______________ year in India it rains for six months.
15. _______________ people work in a *busy* city.

Ending Sentences with Punctuation

A sentence always ends with one of three punctuation marks:

a period (.)   a question mark (?)   an exclamation point (!)

A statement, a command, or a polite request ends with a period (.).

Zane picks up his toys. (*statement*)   Go in the third door. (*command*)

Please forgive me. (*request*)

A question ends with a question mark (?).

Why did you do that?   Where are my keys?

An exclamation is a shout. It ends with an exclamation point (!). A command can, too.

It looks like it's going to rain! (*exclamation*)

Do not slam the door! (*command*)

Other punctuation marks are used inside sentences. They cannot end a sentence:

comma (,)   a semicolon (;)   a colon (:)   a dash (–)

Directions: Put the right punctuation mark at the end of each sentence.

Example: My mom baked an apple pie [.]

1. Her best friend is Erika [ ]
2. Quit being such a pest [ ]
3. Clean the sink [ ]
4. Is he friends with Kyle [ ]
5. We went to Dallas yesterday [ ]
6. What is your phone number [ ]
7. Please answer the question [ ]
8. Where did you put my coat [ ]

Ending Sentences with Punctuation

Directions: Put the right punctuation mark at the end of each sentence.

Example: Let go of that [!]

1. Were my eyes playing tricks on me [ ]
2. Chloe went out in the rain to look for her lost cat [ ]
3. Wow, that's awful [ ]
4. She lifted the box's lid and peeked inside [ ]
5. Wait for me [ ]
6. Are you sure it's safe [ ]
7. In Alaska, it is cold most of the time [ ]
8. Everyone was shocked when shy Kate stepped out onto the stage [ ]
9. I'm so scared [ ]
10. Mike searched in the boxes [ ]
11. Was the bear cub near our tent [ ]
12. Why would anyone steal that old hat [ ]
13. Drew climbs up into the tree house every day [ ]
14. Get away from those flames [ ]
15. How much does this cost [ ]

Writing Sentences

It is easy to write a sentence. All you need is a subject and a verb.

Marcie slept. *subject:* Marcie *verb:* slept

Most sentences have more than two words. They give more information and details.

Marcie slept for two hours. *subject:* Marcie *verb:* slept
details: for two hours

Directions: Use the subject, verb, and details given to write a sentence. Start with a capital letter and use end punctuation. You may need to add words to make the sentences. An example has been done for you.

	Subject	Verb	Details	Your Sentence
ex.	bunny	hid	under steps	The bunny hid under the steps.
1.	I	won	third prize	
2.	bees	buzzed	around flower	
3.	Steven	wants	hamster	
4.	boy	sat	by door	
5.	dog	chews	shoes	
6.	Emily	has	flu	
7.	friend	ran	down street	
8.	they	looked	purse	
9.	bear	ate	honey	
10.	Adam	play	hide and seek	

Writing Sentences

Directions: Use the subject, verb, and details given to write a sentence. Start with a capital letter and use end punctuation. You may need to add words to make the sentences. An example has been done for you.

	Subject	Verb	Details	Your Sentence
ex.	we	can play	board game	We can play a board game.
1.	dad	made	pie	
2.	they	meet	Friday	
3.	horse	followed	path home	
4.	you	do like	cartoons	
5.	oranges	taste	sweet	
6.	I	like	birds	
7.	brother	wrote	story	
8.	storm	wrecked	house	
9.	she	was singing	favorite song	
10.	book	fell	on ground	
11.	fishing	is	fun	
12.	he	wore	red hat	

Asking Questions

If you read a sentence that answers a question, you can figure out what the question might have been. How? **Some of the words in the answer were probably in the question.** For example:

The students are studying.

The question might have to do with what the students are doing. Or, maybe the question has to do with who is doing the studying. Possible questions include:

What are the students doing? Who is studying?

Directions: Draw a line to match the answer to its question. The first one has been done for you.

This Sentence	Answers this Question
1. My best friend is Ava.	Where did Joey go last week? (a)
2. We go bowling each Saturday.	Why wasn't Jessie at your house? (b)
3. The dog ran away.	When was their baby born? (c)
4. Yes, I will come to your party.	How much money did she spend? (d)
5. There are no gifts in the closet.	What did the dog do? (e)
6. They should turn left at the light.	How often do you go bowling? (f)
7. She spent $5.67 on lunch.	Did Zahara find something? (g)
8. Mr. Bud's class has 26 students.	Who is your best friend? (h)
9. Joey went to visit his grandparents.	Is there a gift in there? (i)
10. Jessie had gone for a walk.	Which way should they go? (j)
11. She found a purse in the parking lot.	Will you come to my party? (k)
12. Quinn was born on March 4th.	How many students are in that class? (l)

Asking Questions

Directions: Read each sentence. It is an answer to a question. Figure out what the question might have been. Write it on the line. Use a capital letter and end punctuation.

Example: We ate out on Thursday.

When did you eat out? *OR* What did you do on Thursday?

1. Your notebook is on the desk. ______________________________

____

2. My class eats lunch at 12:30 p.m. ______________________________

____

3. We went to New York City for vacation. ______________________

____

4. I chose the red balloon. ______________________________

____

5. Ben has twelve video games. ______________________________

____

6. The panda bear is Billy's favorite zoo animal. _________________

____

7. The doll cost $38.45. ______________________________

____

8. The parade will come down this street. ______________________

____

9. Yes, Marcus went to the library. ______________________________

____

10. They bought a new car last week. ______________________________

____

Answering Questions

Sometimes you are asked a question. You should answer in a complete sentence. **It's easy—just use the words from the question in your answer.**

Example: What color do you dislike the most?

I dislike the color gray because it seems gloomy.

The writer used the verb *dislike*, the noun *color*, and the adjective *most* in the answer.

Example: Where did Beth go last weekend?

Last weekend Beth went to the beach.

The writer used the nouns *Beth* and *weekend* and the adjective *last* in the answer.

(Notice that the verbs *did* and *go* changed to *went*.)

Directions: Answer each question with a complete sentence.

1. Where do you want to live when you grow up? ______________________________

____

2. When do you like to be outside? ______________________________

____

3. Who is the youngest person in your family? ______________________________

____

4. Why do you brush your teeth? ______________________________

____

5. How old are you? ______________________________

____

6. What is your favorite game? ______________________________

____

Answering Questions

Directions: Answer each question with a complete sentence.

1. When do you eat dinner? ______________________________

   ____

2. Where do you leave your shoes at night? ______________________________

   ____

3. How many months away is your birthday? ______________________________

   ____

4. Who washes the clothes in your home? ______________________________

   ____

5. What is your favorite food? ______________________________

   ____

6. What is your bedtime? ______________________________

   ____

7. Where have you gone on vacation? ______________________________

   ____

8. Who is your best friend? ______________________________

   ____

9. What sport do you like to play? ______________________________

   ____

10. Do you ever skip eating breakfast? ______________________________

    ____

Avoiding Incomplete Sentences

An incomplete sentence is not a sentence because it is an incomplete thought. It may start with a capital letter. It may end with a period, question mark, or exclamation point. But if it is not a complete thought, it is not a sentence.

Incomplete sentence: Since it is Tuesday.

Sentence: Since it is Tuesday, our trash will get picked up.

An incomplete sentence leaves you wondering. A sentence says something you can understand.

Directions: Read each group of words. Write **I** on the line if it is an incomplete sentence. Write **S** on the line if it is a sentence.

________ 1. On Thursday Mrs. Van's class.

________ 2. Everyone stood at the ship's rail.

________ 3. His dad took a photo.

________ 4. If you will.

________ 5. Ashley went to the zoo.

________ 6. I do not know.

________ 7. Who did this?

________ 8. On the grass by the pond.

________ 9. Jeanie's dog's name was Clue.

________ 10. When we get to the park.

Avoiding Incomplete Sentences

Directions: Read each incomplete sentence. Then, add information to make it a complete sentence. Write your new sentence on the line.

Example: After school let out.

After school let out, I ran all the way home.

1. Tell me about. ______________________

____

2. A scary. ______________________

____

3. Ran out of the field. ______________________

____

4. My best friend. ______________________

____

5. How do you? ______________________

____

6. Come on, let's. ______________________

____

7. Forgot my lunch money. ______________________

____

8. Watch out for! ______________________

____

9. Three people on a raft. ______________________

____

10. Smiles a lot. ______________________

____

Avoiding Run-on Sentences

A run-on sentence is two sentences that run together. One way to fix a run-on sentence is to split it into two sentences. When you do this, each sentence needs an end punctuation mark.

Run-on sentence: Andy ate three sandwiches he always eats a lot.

Two sentences: Andy ate three sandwiches. He always eats a lot.

A run-on sentence is hard to read. You gasp for breath because there is no pause. Often, a run-on sentence is two sentences joined with a comma. The comma is where the end punctuation mark should be.

Directions: Read each group of words. Write **S** on the line if it is a sentence. Write **R** on the line if it is a run-on sentence.

Example: R I just got a new video game, wait until you see it!

_______ 1. Rain poured from the clouds we ran for cover.

_______ 2. No one watched TV during dinner at our house.

_______ 3. My sister hid my present, she put it behind the fridge.

_______ 4. Where did you put your boots where did you leave your coat?

_______ 5. My mom overcooked the turkey it still tasted good.

_______ 6. We always trim our tree on Christmas Eve.

_______ 7. Mika likes Mondays because she enjoys going to school.

_______ 8. Turn left on Oak Street, go to the orange house.

_______ 9. While we are still asleep, our dad goes to work each morning.

_______ 10. Why didn't he mail your letter?

_______ 11. My next-door neighbors are nice they have four children.

_______ 12. I wanted to check out the book, but I did not have my library card.

Avoiding Run-on Sentences

Directions: Read each run-on sentence. Then, add punctuation to split it into two sentences. Start both sentences with a capital letter. Write your new sentences on the line.

Example: We have a maple tree that I climb its branches are easy to reach.

We have a maple tree that I climb. Its branches are easy to reach.

1. My coach wants us to win this game, he will be upset if we don't!

    ___

    ___

2. He cried all the way home, I think he was scared.

    ___

    ___

3. My best friend Hannah moved away last month I really miss her.

    ___

    ___

4. Kevin had a swimming pool put in his yard, do you want to go see it?

    ___

    ___

5. The children were excited they talked and laughed on the way there.

    ___

    ___

Joining Sentences

You can join two related sentences together with the conjunctions *and*, *but*, and *or*. *Note:* Using conjunctions is also another way to fix run-on sentences.

The mail has already come + but + You did not get a letter

sentence + conjunction + sentence

(and, but, or)

When you join two sentences with a conjunction, you need a comma before the conjunction.

The mail has already come, but you did not get a letter.

Directions: Join each pair of sentences using one of these conjunctions: *and*, *but*, *or*. Write the new sentence. Put a comma before the conjunction.

Example: Harry planted some flower seeds. Weeds grew instead.

Harry planted some flower seeds, but weeds grew instead.

1. Eric chose a puzzle. Andrew chose a game. ____________________

____

2. Jordan has a red bike. Logan has a green bike. ____________________

____

3. Is Jake going to our school next year? Is he moving before September?

____

____

4. Pam likes wrapping gifts. Saki gets hers wrapped at the store.

____

____

5. Do you like your new shoes? Were your old shoes more comfortable?

____

____

Joining Sentences

Directions: Join each pair of sentences using one of these conjunctions: *and*, *but*, *or*. Write the new sentence. Put a comma before the conjunction.

1. The test was hard. Jake had not studied for it. ______________________

2. Our class pet is a mouse. I like frogs better. ______________________

3. Tamika can go for a walk. She cannot go as far as the ice rink.

4. The president gave a long speech on TV. I missed my favorite show.

5. Should we turn here? Should we keep going in this direction?

6. You must turn in the books today. Tomorrow you will owe late fees.

Editing Sentences

When you edit, you make your writing better. So, after you write something, read it. Be sure you have complete sentences. Check to be sure that none of them are incomplete or run-ons.

Directions: Read each group of words. Mark sentences with an **S**. Mark incomplete sentences with an **I**. Mark run-ons with an **R**.

Example: __I__ Is that store?

________ 1. Emily asked Tony where her pen was.

________ 2. The fire fighters.

________ 3. In a big brown box.

________ 4. Do you like your new car?

________ 5. The cell phone was.

________ 6. Having a great time.

________ 7. The news reports were wrong, the story was not true.

________ 8. She got a new cage for her bird.

________ 9. We have gym, art, and music each week, I like art best.

________ 10. Thanksgiving and the Fourth of July are the best holidays.

________ 11. The wind in their faces.

________ 12. Please forgive me, I will fix the mistake right now.

________ 13. If they go to the mall today.

________ 14. Melissa is too excited to sleep, her birthday party is tomorrow.

________ 15. Let's do the first draft now we can edit it after lunch.

Editing Sentences

Directions: Read each group of words. Some are sentences, some are incomplete sentences, and some are run-ons. If it is a sentence, leave it alone. If it is an incomplete sentence, write it on the line with extra information to make it complete. If it is a run-on sentence, write it on the line with punctuation and a capital letter.

Example: The waves and the wind.

The waves and the wind made our boat tip.

1. A new crate for the puppy. ____________________

____

2. Come over to my house, we will have ice cream cones.

____

____

3. My mom said if I cleaned my room, I could go to the new movie.

____

____

4. That stamp belonged to my grandpa it is old and very valuable.

____

____

5. Since last year.

____

____

6. Alexa does not want any tea she says it is too hot.

____

____

Assessment: Sentence Types and Punctuation

Directions: Read each sentence. Decide if it is a statement, a question, a command, or an exclamation. Then, darken the correct circle.

1. What a cute kitten!
   Ⓐ statement Ⓑ question Ⓒ command/request Ⓓ exclamation

2. Is it raining now?
   Ⓐ statement Ⓑ question Ⓒ command/request Ⓓ exclamation

3. Please eat the carrots.
   Ⓐ statement Ⓑ question Ⓒ command/request Ⓓ exclamation

4. I want to play a card game.
   Ⓐ statement Ⓑ question Ⓒ command/request Ⓓ exclamation

5. He made a cake for her birthday.
   Ⓐ statement Ⓑ question Ⓒ command/request Ⓓ exclamation

Directions: Read each sentence. Decide what kind of sentence it is. Then, darken the circle to show the correct end punctuation.

6. Watch out ☐
   Ⓐ . Ⓑ ? Ⓒ !

7. Does your dog bite ☐
   Ⓐ . Ⓑ ? Ⓒ !

8. They will leave next week ☐
   Ⓐ . Ⓑ ? Ⓒ !

9. Will you come to see me tomorrow ☐
   Ⓐ . Ⓑ ? Ⓒ !

10. Hurry up ☐
    Ⓐ . Ⓑ ? Ⓒ !

Assessment: Errors and Sentence Parts

Directions: Read each sentence. Decide if it is fine as it is or if it can be improved. Then, darken the correct circle.

1. Did you find it hard to fall asleep
   - ⓐ needs a capital letter
   - ⓑ needs punctuation
   - ⓒ subject and verb need to agree
   - ⓓ fine as it is

2. put your name on your paper.
   - ⓐ needs a capital letter
   - ⓑ needs punctuation
   - ⓒ subject and verb need to agree
   - ⓓ fine as it is

3. Joe and Tom goes to your house every weekend.
   - ⓐ needs a capital letter
   - ⓑ needs punctuation
   - ⓒ subject and verb need to agree
   - ⓓ fine as it is

4. My cat likes to eat tuna
   - ⓐ needs a capital letter
   - ⓑ needs punctuation
   - ⓒ subject and verb need to agree
   - ⓓ fine as it is

5. The flock of birds fly high.
   - ⓐ needs a capital letter
   - ⓑ needs punctuation
   - ⓒ subject and verb need to agree
   - ⓓ fine as it is

Directions: Read each sentence. Decide what kind of word is underlined. Then, darken the correct circle.

6. They called all of the people on the list.
   ⓐ subject ⓑ verb ⓒ preposition ⓓ article

7. The horse ran very fast.
   ⓐ subject ⓑ verb ⓒ preposition ⓓ article

8. Let's not fight about this.
   ⓐ subject ⓑ verb ⓒ preposition ⓓ article

9. My mom bought a new car.
   ⓐ subject ⓑ verb ⓒ preposition ⓓ article

10. The hill was too steep to climb.
    ⓐ subject ⓑ verb ⓒ preposition ⓓ article

Assessment: Tri-Sentence Review

Directions: Read each group of words. Decide if it is an incomplete sentence, a sentence, or a run-on. Then, darken the correct circle.

1. On a dark, stormy night.
   ⓐ incomplete sentence ⓑ sentence ⓒ run-on sentence

2. She burned her arm.
   ⓐ incomplete sentence ⓑ sentence ⓒ run-on sentence

3. We are going to play a game do you want to play, too?
   ⓐ incomplete sentence ⓑ sentence ⓒ run-on sentence

4. I got a new skateboard it is red and black and goes fast.
   ⓐ incomplete sentence ⓑ sentence ⓒ run-on sentence

5. Myla is the short girl with black hair.
   ⓐ incomplete sentence ⓑ sentence ⓒ run-on sentence

6. My sandwich tastes bad may I share yours?
   ⓐ incomplete sentence ⓑ sentence ⓒ run-on sentence

7. Brad frowned.
   ⓐ incomplete sentence ⓑ sentence ⓒ run-on sentence

8. Sit over there.
   ⓐ incomplete sentence ⓑ sentence ⓒ run-on sentence

9. Telling me a story.
   ⓐ incomplete sentence ⓑ sentence ⓒ run-on sentence

10. When it stops.
    ⓐ incomplete sentence ⓑ sentence ⓒ run-on sentence

Answer Key

page 4

1. O 2. N 3. A 4. T 5. O
6. S 7. N 8. T 9. S 10. A

page 5

1. N 2. T 3. A 4. O 5. S
6. O 7. T 8. A 9. S 10. N

Answers will vary but may be similar to:
My favorite color is (color).
Will you give me a ride to school? *OR*
May I have a ride to school?
Stop bugging me. *OR* Quit bugging me.

page 6

1. Q 2. C 3. E 4. S 5. E 6. C 7. Q 8. S

page 7

statement: 3, 6; question: 2, 8; command: 1, 5
exclamation: 4, 7
Answers will vary but may be similar to:
I live at (address).
Will you play a board game with me?
Pick up the toys.
I like (name)!

page 8

1. Ben opened the door.
2. Did you go to the fair?
3. Call the dog. **You**
4. Shut the windows. **You**
5. Sara laid the book on her bed.
6. Fairport is one of the towns along the river.

page 9

1. We raced to the finish line.
2. What did Bailey say?
3. They sang loudly.
4. A thick forest blocked our view of the shore.
5. Did Dan watch a movie?
6. Turn down the TV. **You**
7. Liz pulled a chair up to the table.
8. I just saw a falling star!
9. They slept well last night.
10. Does she like it?
11. Eat up! **You**
12. Sit down over there. **You**
13. Your shoe is dirty.
14. Did you read the book?
15. Make some hot cocoa. **You**

page 10

1. P 2. S 3. S 4. S 5. P 6. S 7. P 8. P

page 11

1. D 2. A 3. A 4. D 5. D 6. A 7. D 8. A

Answers will vary, but the verb must be as shown:

Subject	Verb	Sentence
boys	talk(s)	The boys talk to their sister.
she	write(s)	She **writes** to her friend.
they	stop(s)	They **stop** at the light.
we	like(s)	We **like** ice cream.
flock	rest(s)	The flock **rests** near the pond.
mother	laugh(s)	My mother **laughs** at the joke.
cats	purr(s)	The cats **purr** when they are hungry.

page 12

1. Music CDs and DVDs can be checked out from the library.
2. Where are my pencil and paper? (verb changed when it became a compound subject)
3. Kara and Tim like to play with trucks. (verb changed when it became a compound subject)
4. Did Jim or Megan come home late?
5. My sister and brother ran in the race.

page 13

Answers will vary but may be similar to:

1. Both (Name and Name) got done early.
2. Were (Name and Name) planning to go to his party?
3. (Name and Name) are good friends with Rico.
4. My (name and name) bought me a new bike.
5. (Name and Name) are three years old.
6. How did (Name and Name) find their way out?
7. His (name and name) enjoy playing chess.
8. (Name and Name) were born in March.
9. The (item and item) are in the cabinet.
10. What happened to her (item and item *OR* name and name)?
11. (Name and Name) own cell phones.
12. The (item and item) are far from Earth.
13. (Sport and sport) are my two favorite sports.
14. Conner's (item and item *OR* name and name) got hurt in the crash.
15. Where did (Name and Name) go last night?

page 14

1. Zack cleared and set the table.
2. Will Jill rake the yard and trim the bushes?
3. Josh tripped on a root and dropped the bag.
4. Did Karli feed and walk the dog?
5. Mason ran to the door and opened it.
6. Matt sat down and played the game.

page 15

1. Will Candi cook and serve the meal?
2. The tree branch snapped and crashed to the ground.
3. I ate a meal but still feel hungry!

Answer Key *(cont.)*

4. The woman smiled and waved at them.
5. People stopped and watched the boy on the skateboard.
6. Can you sing and skip rope at the same time?

Sentences will vary.

page 16

1. Please do not put the box on that chair.
2. I wish you could come with me to the party.
3. Do you have the book that Matt lent you?
4. An apple pie was on the table.
5. Let's buy an ice cream cone after the show ends.
6. A boat was tied to the dock.
7. The new toy was broken in less than two days.
8. Where do you keep the forks?
9. Step on the gas!
10. An axe was lying on the ground.

page 17

1. A/The dog chewed on an/the old bone.
2. Will you come to the library with me?
3. After all the leaves fell, we raked them into a big pile.
4. I went on the/a field trip to the/an apple orchard.
5. We built a/the snowman in the front yard.
6. An/The animal had dug the/a hole by the/a bush.
7. Frank tried to find the/an exit.
8. She gets paid on the first day of each month.
9. You need an egg to make this cake.
10. What time of day did the fire start?
11. The boy was happy to get the/a gift.
12. He can open the lock with the/a key.
13. Take the clothes out of the dryer.
14. Is a/the cat hiding under the bed?
15. Jack found a/the cell phone in a/the ditch.

page 18

1. We sat on a bench in the park after the wedding.
2. Of all the songs we sang, I liked that one the best.
3. Pick up the plates and put them by the sink.
4. The cat was lying above the chair.
5. She was named after her mother.
6. Ali went to the store with Jen.
7. At the museum, Cody got a poster about jets.
8. The farmer put the pig back into its pen.

page 19

1. under	2. up	3. from	4. in
5. with	6. at	7. into	8. by
9. of	10. on	11. about	12. to

page 20

1. My older brother plays football.
2. I wore a blue wig with my costume.
3. Did you see that striped car?
4. We watched a great movie on Saturday.
5. His little sister sings in the chorus.
6. Seth is the third child in the family.
7. Is Mrs. Frank a short woman?
8. I asked for a new skateboard for my birthday.
9. Those socks are ugly!
10. Clouds filled the dark sky.
11. What is the biggest box you have?
12. Look at that cute puppy!

page 21

Answers will vary but may be similar to:

1. dirty, muddy, filthy, etc.
2. scared, frightened, young, small, little, etc.
3. pumpkin, apple, peach, cherry, raspberry, chocolate, mince, etc.
4. little, big, pretty, noisy, (any color), etc.
5. stray, small, big, old, smelly, etc.
6. baked, mashed, fried, cheesy, au gratin, scalloped, etc.
7. apple, grape, orange, cranberry, etc.
8. young, scared, little, etc.
9. front, back, side, car, barn, cabin, etc.
10. fuzzy, warm, little, new, (any color), etc.
11. metal, glass, cake, brownie, (any color), etc.
12. tallest, shortest, smartest, nicest, meanest, etc.
13. old, rotten, (any tree), etc.
14. new, old, pretty, ugly, haunted, (any color), etc.
15. left, right, injured, etc.

page 22

1. Is your grandpa tall?
2. He has a big nose.
3. The frying pan was not warm.
4. It is already time to go.
5. Did that boy run fast?
6. Which book comes after this one?
7. The wind blew hard.
8. What is his name?

page 23

1. We ate meat and rice. *OR*
   We ate rice and meat.
2. What did you just say?
3. How did she cut her arm?
4. You were able to tame the wild bird.
5. Would you like to meet my sister?
6. She came to the class early. *OR*
   She came early to the class.
7. Did his dad fix the broken wheel?

Answer Key *(cont.)*

8. They came home yesterday. *OR* Yesterday they came home.
9. My printer has run out of ink.
10. The color of the den is yellow. *OR* Yellow is the color of the den.
11. Did you read the book by yourself?
12. He won the race this afternoon. *OR* This afternoon he won the race.

page 24

Answers will vary. Typical ones are:

1. The
2. I, We, You, He, She, They, (Name)
3. Last
4. My, Our, Your, His, Her, Their, This, That, The, (Name)
5. Please
6. I, We, You, He, She, They, (Name)
7. Would
8. My, Our, Your, His, Her, Their, (Name)
9. Did
10. Has, Did
11. Let's
12. You
13. To
14. Is
15. Next, This

page 25

1. That	2. Do	3. What	4. We
5. When	6. My	7. Few	8. He
9. How	10. Have	11. Look	12. Please
13. Where	14. Each	15. Many	

page 26

1. .   2. !   3. .   4. ?   5. .   6. ?   7. .   8. ?

page 27

1. ?	2. .	3. !	4. .
5. !	6. ?	7. .	8. .
9. !	10. .	11. ?	12. ?
13. .	14. !	15. ?	

page 28

Answers will vary but may be similar to:

1. I won third prize.
2. Some bees buzzed around the flower.
3. Steven wants a hamster.
4. A boy sat by the door.
5. My dog chews on shoes.
6. Emily has the flu.
7. (My, His, Her, Our, Their) friend ran down the street.
8. They looked for the purse.
9. The bear ate the honey.
10. Adam plays hide and seek.

page 29

Answers will vary but may be similar to:

1. My dad made a pie.
2. They meet every Friday.
3. The horse followed the path home.
4. You do like cartoons. *OR* Do you like cartoons?
5. The oranges taste sweet.
6. I like birds.
7. His brother wrote the story.
8. The storm wrecked the house.
9. She was singing her favorite song.
10. Her book fell on the ground.
11. Fishing is fun! *OR* Is fishing fun?
12. He wore a red hat.

page 30

1. My best friend is Ava. (h. Who is your best friend?)
2. We go bowling each Saturday. (f. How often do you go bowling?)
3. The dog ran away. (e. What did the dog do?)
4. Yes, I will come to your party. (k. Will you come to my party?)
5. There are no gifts in the closet. (i. Is there a gift in there?)
6. They should turn left at the light. (j. Which way should they go?)
7. She spent $5.67 on lunch. (d. How much money did she spend?)
8. Mr. Bud's class has 26 students. (l. How many students are in that class?)
9. Joey went to visit his grandparents. (a. Where did Joey go last week?)
10. Jessie had gone for a walk. (b. Why wasn't Jessie at your house?)
11. She found a purse in the parking lot. (g. Did Zahara find something?)
12. Quinn was born on March 4th. (c. When was their baby born?)

page 31

Answers will vary but may be similar to:

1. Where is my notebook? *OR* What is on the desk?
2. When does your class eat lunch?
3. Where did you go for vacation?
4. Which balloon did you choose? *OR* What did you choose?
5. How many video games does Ben have?
6. What is Billy's favorite zoo animal? *OR* What animal did Billy like best at the zoo?
7. How much did the doll cost? *OR* What was the price of the doll?
8. Will the parade come down this street? *OR* Where will the parade go? *OR* What street will the parade go down?

Answer Key *(cont.)*

9. Did Marcus go to the library?
10. What did they buy last week? *OR* When did they buy a new car?

page 32

Answers will vary, but they should be worded like this:

1. I want to live (place) when I grow up.
2. I like to be outside (time, season, or weather conditions).
3. The youngest person in my family is (Name).
4. I brush my teeth because (reason).
5. I am (age) years old.
6. My favorite game is (name of game).

page 33

Answers will vary, but they should be worded like this:

1. I eat dinner at (time).
2. I leave my shoes (place) at night.
3. My birthday is (number) months away.
4. (Name) washes the clothes in my home.
5. My favorite food is (food).
6. My bedtime is (time).
7. I have gone to (location) on vacation.
8. My best friend is (Name).
9. I like to play (sport or activity).
10. Yes, I skip eating breakfast (how often). *OR* No, I never skip eating breakfast.

page 34

1. I	2. S	3. S	4. I	5. S
6. S	7. S	8. I	9. S	10. I

page 35

Answers will vary but may be similar to:

1. Tell me about (something or Name).
2. A scary (something) (verb). *OR* I/(Name) (verb) a scary (something).
3. (Something or Name) ran out of the field.
4. My best friend (verb) (something or Name).
5. How do you (verb)?
6. Come on, let's (verb).
7. *I* forgot my lunch money.
8. Watch out for (something)!
9. Three people on a raft (verb) (something or name). *OR* (Something or name) (verb) three people on a raft.
10. (Name) smiles a lot.

page 36

1. R	2. S	3. R	4. R	5. R	6. S
7. S	8. R	9. S	10. S	11. R	12. S

page 37

1. My coach wants us to win this game. He will be upset if we don't!
2. He cried all the way home. I think he was scared.
3. My best friend Hannah moved away last month. I really miss her.
4. Kevin had a swimming pool put in his yard. Do you want to go see it?
5. The children were excited. They talked and laughed on the way there.

page 38

1. Eric chose a puzzle, *and* Andrew chose a game.
2. Jordan has a red bike, *and* Logan has a green bike.
3. Is Jake going to our school next year, *or* is he moving before September?
4. Pam likes wrapping gifts, *but* Saki gets hers wrapped at the store.
5. Do you like your new shoes, *or* were your old shoes more comfortable?

page 39

1. The test was hard, *and* Jake had not studied for it.
2. Our class pet is a mouse, *but* I like frogs better.
3. Tamika can go for a walk, *but* she cannot go as far as the ice rink.
4. The president gave a long speech on TV, *and* I missed my favorite show.
5. Should we turn here, *or* should we keep going in this direction?
6. You must turn in the books today, *or* tomorrow you will owe late fees.

page 40

1. S	2. I	3. I	4. S	5. I
6. I	7. R	8. S	9. R	10. S
11. I	12. R	13. I	14. R	15. R

page 41

Answers will vary but may be similar to:

1. We got a new crate for the puppy. (was incomplete)
2. Come over to my house. We will have ice cream cones. (was a run-on)
3. This one did not need repair. It was already a sentence.
4. That stamp belonged to my grandpa. It is old and very valuable. (was a run-on)
5. Since last year, I have grown three inches. (was incomplete)
6. Alexa does not want any tea. She says it is too hot. (was a run-on)

page 42

1. d	2. b	3. c	4. a	5. a
6. c	7. b	8. a	9. b	10. c

page 43

1. b	2. a	3. c	4. b	5. c
6. c	7. d	8. b	9. a	10. a

page 44

1. a	2. b	3. c	4. c	5. b
6. c	7. b	8. b	9. a	10. a

Made in the USA
Monee, IL
18 October 2022